the NLT
BIBLE
PROMISE
BOOK
for women

Tyndale House Publishers, Inc., Carol Stream, Illinois

Visit Tyndale's exciting Web site at www.tyndale.com.

TYNDALE, New Living Translation, NLT, the New Living Translation logo, and Tyndale's quill logo are registered trademarks of Tyndale House Publishers, Inc.

The NLT Bible Promise Book for Women

Copyright © 2010 by Ronald A. Beers. All rights reserved.

Designed by Jennifer Ghionzoli

Compiled and edited by Amy E. Mason. All rights reserved.

Scripture quotations are taken from the *Holy Bible,* New Living Translation, copyright © 1996, 2004, 2007 by Tyndale House Foundation. Used by permission of Tyndale House Publishers, Inc., Carol Stream, Illinois 60188. All rights reserved.

ISBN 978-1-4143-3775-3

Printed in the United States of America

16   15   14   13   12   11   10
7   6   5   4   3   2

❧ CONTENTS ❧

Today, most women live in a world of opportunity. We have freedoms, rights, and abilities that women before us never dared to dream of. But with all these opportunities come many confusing situations, and often we find ourselves overwhelmed, not knowing which opportunities are best and which decisions are right. Knowing the endless possibilities can make us keenly aware and afraid of the unknown. You may sometimes wish that you had a starting point on which to build your life, something to guide your decision making in a consistent fashion. Wouldn't it be nice to be assured of what is true and good, what to avoid, and what your future holds?

The Bible is full of such assurances. God's promises offer guidance, protection, and truth as we strive to make the most of life. They reveal his plans for all of creation and for you and me. They also teach us how to live out these promises, what we must do in order to receive God's blessings in our lives, and how to receive comfort and confidence as we face the unknown.

This little book is arranged by topic to guide you in your moments of curiosity or deepest need. Topics were chosen that are most relevant to the issues, concerns, and desires women face, with Bible promises to help you live out your faith with obedience, joy, and confidence. Every verse is drawn from the easy to read and understand New Living Translation. There are nearly 150 promises in this book to help you cope with life's difficulties and celebrate the blessings of walking with God. As you realize the power of God's promises in your life, you will have the strength and guidance to make decisions consistent with God's purposes and to build your life upon his eternal Word.

ABANDONMENT

When God feels far away . . .

The LORD will not abandon his people, because that would dishonor his great name. For it has pleased the LORD to make you his very own people.

1 Samuel 12:22

Even if my father and mother abandon me, the LORD will hold me close.

Psalm 27:10

No, I will not abandon you as orphans—I will come to you.

John 14:18

God has said, "I will never fail you. I will never abandon you."

Hebrews 13:5

ABILITIES

When you wonder if God has given you any significant abilities . . .

In his grace, God has given us different gifts for doing certain things well.
Romans 12:6

A spiritual gift is given to each of us.
1 Corinthians 12:7

When you're not sure how to use your abilities . . .

These . . . gifts Christ gave to the church . . . to equip God's people to do his work and build up the church, the body of Christ . . . until we all come to such unity in our faith and knowledge of God's Son that we will be mature in the Lord, measuring up to the full and complete standard of Christ.
Ephesians 4:11-13

When your limitations cause you to doubt your ability to serve God well . . .

It is not by force nor by strength, but by my Spirit, says the LORD of Heaven's Armies.
Zechariah 4:6

ACCEPTANCE

When you need to know that God accepts you as you are . . .

Nothing in all creation will ever be able to separate us from the love of God that is revealed in Christ Jesus our Lord.
Romans 8:39

He has reconciled you to himself through the death of Christ. . . . As a result, he has brought you into his own presence, and you are holy and blameless as you stand before him without a single fault.
Colossians 1:22

AGING

When you fear growing older . . .

The glory of the young is their strength; the gray hair of experience is the splendor of the old.
Proverbs 20:29

I will be your God throughout your lifetime—until your hair is white with age. I made you, and I will care for you. I will carry you along and save you.
Isaiah 46:4

When you want to make the most of every moment . . .

Store my commands in your heart. If you do this . . . your life will be satisfying.
Proverbs 3:1-2

Fear of the LORD lengthens one's life, but the years of the wicked are cut short.
Proverbs 10:27

ANGELS

When you wonder if angels are involved in the world today . . .

The angel of the LORD is a guard; he surrounds and defends all who fear him.
Psalm 34:7

Don't forget to show hospitality to strangers, for some who have done this have entertained angels without realizing it!
Hebrews 13:2

ANGER

When you're afraid God is angry with you . . .

His anger lasts only a moment, but his favor lasts a lifetime!
Psalm 30:5

The LORD is compassionate and merciful, slow to get angry and filled with unfailing love.
Psalm 103:8

When you can't stop feeling angry . . .

[Love] is not irritable, and it keeps no record of being wronged.
1 Corinthians 13:5

Make allowance for each other's faults, and forgive anyone who offends you. Remember, the Lord forgave you, so you must forgive others. Above all, clothe yourselves with love, which binds us all together in perfect harmony. And let the peace that comes from Christ rule in your hearts.
Colossians 3:13-15

When someone is angry with you . . .

A gentle answer deflects anger, but harsh words make
tempers flare.

  Proverbs 15:1

Don't repay evil for evil. Don't retaliate with insults when
people insult you. Instead, pay them back with a blessing.
That is what God has called you to do, and he will bless you
for it.

  1 Peter 3:9

⚮ ASSURANCE

When you need to know God is still in charge . . .

For that is what God is like. He is our God forever and ever,
and he will guide us until we die.

  Psalm 48:14

All the nations you made will come and bow before you,
Lord; they will praise your holy name.

  Psalm 86:9

I hold you by your right hand—I, the LORD your God. And
I say to you, "Don't be afraid. I am here to help you."

  Isaiah 41:13

When you're not sure God holds you in his hand . . .

I give them eternal life, and they will never perish. No one
can snatch them away from me, for my Father has given them
to me, and he is more powerful than anyone else. No one can
snatch them from the Father's hand.

  John 10:28-29

When you don't feel anyone notices . . .

People judge by outward appearance, but the LORD looks at the heart.

1 Samuel 16:7

You made all the delicate, inner parts of my body and knit me together in my mother's womb. Thank you for making me so wonderfully complex! . . . You watched me as I was being formed . . . as I was woven together in the dark of the womb. You saw me before I was born. Every day of my life was recorded in your book. Every moment was laid out before a single day had passed. How precious are your thoughts about me, O God. They cannot be numbered!

Psalm 139:13-17

When you're unsure of your salvation . . .

Everyone who calls on the name of the LORD will be saved.

Acts 2:21

If you confess with your mouth that Jesus is Lord and believe in your heart that God raised him from the dead, you will be saved.

Romans 10:9

We know he lives in us because the Spirit he gave us lives in us.

1 John 3:24

BELONGING

When you wonder if there is a place for you to serve . . .

Just as our bodies have many parts and each part has a special function, so it is with Christ's body. We are many parts of one body, and we all belong to each other.

Romans 12:4-5

When you want to know the value of fellowship with Jesus . . .

Remain in me, and I will remain in you. For a branch cannot produce fruit if it is severed from the vine, and you cannot be fruitful unless you remain in me.

John 15:4

You are my friends if you do what I command. I no longer call you slaves, because a master doesn't confide in his slaves. Now you are my friends, since I have told you everything the Father told me.

John 15:14-15

God sent him to buy freedom for us who were slaves to the law, so that he could adopt us as his very own children. And because we are his children, God has sent the Spirit of his Son into our hearts, prompting us to call out, "Abba, Father." Now you are no longer a slave but God's own child. And since you are his child, God has made you his heir.

Galatians 4:5-7

BIBLE

When you wonder if the Bible is relevant . . .

The rain and snow come down from the heavens and stay on
the ground to water the earth. They cause the grain to grow,
producing seed for the farmer and bread for the hungry. It is
the same with my word. I send it out, and it always produces
fruit. It will accomplish all I want it to, and it will prosper
everywhere I send it.
   Isaiah 55:10-11

When I discovered your words, I devoured them. They are my
joy and my heart's delight.
   Jeremiah 15:16

His commands lead to eternal life.
   John 12:50

When you wish God would speak to you . . .

Your laws please me; they give me wise advice.
   Psalm 119:24

All Scripture is inspired by God and is useful to teach us what
is true and to make us realize what is wrong in our lives. It
corrects us when we are wrong and teaches us to do what is
right. God uses it to prepare and equip his people to do every
good work.
   2 Timothy 3:16-17

The word of God is alive and powerful. It is sharper than the
sharpest two-edged sword, cutting between soul and spirit,
between joint and marrow. It exposes our innermost thoughts
and desires.
   Hebrews 4:12

When you need a reminder that God's Word is reliable . . .

The grass withers and the flowers fade, but the word of our God stands forever.

Isaiah 40:8

The Scriptures give us hope and encouragement as we wait patiently for God's promises to be fulfilled.

Romans 15:4

BLESSINGS

When you need to be reminded of all God's blessings . . .

If you fully obey the LORD your God and carefully keep all his commands that I am giving you today, the LORD your God will set you high. . . . Wherever you go and whatever you do, you will be blessed.

Deuteronomy 28:1, 6

The LORD God is our sun and our shield. He gives us grace and glory. The LORD will withhold no good thing from those who do what is right.

Psalm 84:11

All praise to God, the Father of our Lord Jesus Christ, who has blessed us with every spiritual blessing in the heavenly realms because we are united with Christ.

Ephesians 1:3

BUSYNESS

When your schedule is out of control . . .

Teach us to realize the brevity of life, so that we may grow in wisdom.
  Psalm 90:12

When you feel guilty for taking a break . . .

He lets me rest in green meadows; he leads me beside peaceful streams.
  Psalm 23:2

Those who live in the shelter of the Most High will find rest in the shadow of the Almighty.
  Psalm 91:1

CARING

When you wonder if God really cares about your life . . .

I will be glad and rejoice in your unfailing love, for you have seen my troubles, and you care about the anguish of my soul.
  Psalm 31:7

The LORD keeps watch over you as you come and go, both now and forever.
  Psalm 121:8

Give all your worries and cares to God, for he cares about you.
  1 Peter 5:7

CELEBRATION

When you need a reason to celebrate . . .

The LORD your God has blessed you in everything you have done. He has watched your every step.
Deuteronomy 2:7

Let the whole earth sing to the LORD! Each day proclaim the good news that he saves. . . . Give thanks to the LORD, for he is good! His faithful love endures forever.
1 Chronicles 16:23, 34

I trust in your unfailing love. I will rejoice because you have rescued me. I will sing to the LORD because he is good to me.
Psalm 13:5-6

CHANGE

When you're looking for stability in the midst of change . . .

God is our refuge and strength, always ready to help in times of trouble. So we will not fear when earthquakes come and the mountains crumble into the sea.
Psalm 46:1-2

Heaven and earth will disappear, but my words will never disappear.
Mark 13:31

When you need a change but are hesitant . . .

We know that God causes everything to work together for the good of those who love God and are called according to his purpose for them.

Romans 8:28

Don't copy the behavior and customs of this world, but let God transform you into a new person by changing the way you think. Then you will learn to know God's will for you, which is good and pleasing and perfect.

Romans 12:2

I am certain that God, who began the good work within you, will continue his work until it is finally finished on the day when Christ Jesus returns.

Philippians 1:6

When you're moving into a new stage of life . . .

This is my command—be strong and courageous! Do not be afraid or discouraged. For the LORD your God is with you wherever you go.

Joshua 1:9

The godly will flourish like palm trees and grow strong like the cedars of Lebanon. For they are transplanted to the LORD's own house. They flourish in the courts of our God. Even in old age they will still produce fruit; they will remain vital and green.

Psalm 92:12-14

CHARACTER

When your reputation is on the line . . .

Charm is deceptive, and beauty does not last; but a woman who fears the LORD will be greatly praised.
Proverbs 31:30

Don't be concerned about the outward beauty of fancy hairstyles, expensive jewelry, or beautiful clothes. You should clothe yourselves instead with the beauty that comes from within, the unfading beauty of a gentle and quiet spirit, which is so precious to God.
1 Peter 3:3-4

When your integrity is put to the test . . .

We can rejoice, too, when we run into problems and trials, for we know that they help us develop endurance. And endurance develops strength of character, and character strengthens our confident hope of salvation.
Romans 5:3-4

When you long to be more like Jesus . . .

God is working in you, giving you the desire and the power to do what pleases him.
Philippians 2:13

Supplement your faith with a generous provision of moral excellence, and moral excellence with knowledge, and knowledge with self-control, and self-control with patient endurance, and patient endurance with godliness. . . . The more you grow like this, the more productive and useful you will be in your knowledge of our Lord Jesus Christ.

2 Peter 1:5-6, 8

CHILDREN

When you are frustrated with your children . . .

Children are a gift from the LORD; they are a reward from him.

Psalm 127:3

When you wonder how to teach your children about God . . .

Commit yourselves wholeheartedly to these words of mine. Tie them to your hands and wear them on your forehead as reminders. Teach them to your children. Talk about them when you are at home and when you are on the road, when you are going to bed and when you are getting up . . . so that . . . you and your children may flourish.

Deuteronomy 11:18-19, 21

Believe in the Lord Jesus and you will be saved.

Acts 16:31

Be an example . . . in what you say, in the way you live, in your love, your faith, and your purity.

1 Timothy 4:12

When you can't be there to protect your children . . .

The LORD is like a father to his children, tender and
compassionate to those who fear him.

Psalm 103:13

I will pour out my Spirit on your descendants, and my blessing
on your children.

Isaiah 44:3

My Spirit will not leave them, and neither will these words
I have given you. They will be on your lips and on the
lips of your children and your children's children forever.
I, the LORD, have spoken!

Isaiah 59:21

When you get impatient with your children . . .

[Jesus] said to them, "Let the children come to me. Don't stop
them! For the Kingdom of God belongs to those who are like
these children. I tell you the truth, anyone who doesn't receive
the Kingdom of God like a child will never enter it. Then he
took the children in his arms . . . and blessed them."

Mark 10:14-16

CHOICES

When you want God to help you make better choices . . .

Show me the right path, O LORD; point out the road for me
to follow. . . . The LORD is good and does what is right; he
shows the proper path to those who go astray. He leads the
humble in doing right, teaching them his way.

Psalm 25:4, 8-9

I have hidden your word in my heart, that I might not sin against you.
    Psalm 119:11

He guards the paths of the just and protects those who are faithful to him. Then you will understand what is right, just, and fair, and you will find the right way to go. For wisdom will enter your heart, and knowledge will fill you with joy.
    Proverbs 2:8-10

If you need wisdom, ask our generous God, and he will give it to you. He will not rebuke you for asking.
    James 1:5

CHURCH

When you wonder if you should go to church . . .

Where two or three gather together as my followers, I am there among them.
    Matthew 18:20

When it seems your church doesn't need you . . .

He makes the whole body fit together perfectly. As each part does its own special work, it helps the other parts grow, so that the whole body is healthy and growing and full of love.
    Ephesians 4:16

COMFORT

When you need a safe place to go . . .

The LORD is a shelter for the oppressed, a refuge in times
of trouble.
  Psalm 9:9

You are my hiding place; you protect me from trouble.
You surround me with songs of victory.
  Psalm 32:7

When you need to quiet your fears . . .

Even when I walk through the darkest valley, I will not be
afraid, for you are close beside me. Your rod and your staff
protect and comfort me.
  Psalm 23:4

He will feed his flock like a shepherd. He will carry the lambs
in his arms, holding them close to his heart. He will gently
lead the mother sheep with their young.
  Isaiah 40:11

When your heart is torn with grief . . .

He heals the brokenhearted and bandages their wounds.
  Psalm 147:3

God blesses those who mourn, for they will be comforted.
  Matthew 5:4

The Holy Spirit helps us in our weakness. . . . But the Holy
Spirit prays for us with groanings that cannot be expressed
in words.
  Romans 8:26

When there is no one there to console you . . .

You keep track of all my sorrows. You have collected all my tears in your bottle. You have recorded each one in your book.
Psalm 56:8

The LORD is good, a strong refuge when trouble comes. He is close to those who trust in him.
Nahum 1:7

When someone else needs your reassurance . . .

All praise to God, the Father of our Lord Jesus Christ. God is our merciful Father and the source of all comfort. He comforts us in all our troubles so that we can comfort others. When they are troubled, we will be able to give them the same comfort God has given us.
2 Corinthians 1:3-4

∿ CONFIDENCE

When you have doubts about what lies ahead . . .

Those who are righteous will be long remembered. They do not fear bad news; they confidently trust the LORD to care for them.
Psalm 112:6-7

Blessed are those who trust in the LORD and have made the LORD their hope and confidence.
Jeremiah 17:7

I have told you all this so that you may have peace in me. Here on earth you will have many trials and sorrows. But take heart, because I have overcome the world.
John 16:33

When you lose confidence in yourself . . .

The LORD your God is living among you. He is a mighty savior. He will take delight in you with gladness. With his love, he will calm all your fears. He will rejoice over you with joyful songs.

Zephaniah 3:17

You have not received a spirit that makes you fearful slaves. Instead, you received God's Spirit when he adopted you as his own children. Now we call him, "Abba, Father." For his Spirit joins with our spirit to affirm that we are God's children.

Romans 8:15-16

When you want to be sure of your eternal destiny . . .

We are always confident, even though we know that as long as we live in these bodies we are not at home with the Lord. For we live by believing and not by seeing. Yes, we are fully confident, and we would rather be away from these earthly bodies, for then we will be at home with the Lord.

2 Corinthians 5:6-8

When you wonder if your life has any value . . .

How precious are your thoughts about me, O God. They cannot be numbered!

Psalm 139:17

You are no longer a slave but God's own child. And since you are his child, God has made you his heir.

Galatians 4:7

We are God's masterpiece. He has created us anew in Christ Jesus, so we can do the good things he planned for us long ago.

Ephesians 2:10

CONTENTMENT

When you find yourself wanting more . . .

For the despondent, every day brings trouble; for the happy heart, life is a continual feast.

   Proverbs 15:15

True godliness with contentment is itself great wealth.

   1 Timothy 6:6

Don't love money; be satisfied with what you have. For God has said, "I will never fail you. I will never abandon you."

   Hebrews 13:5

By his divine power, God has given us everything we need for living a godly life. We have received all of this by coming to know him, the one who called us to himself by means of his marvelous glory and excellence.

   2 Peter 1:3

COPING

When life is hard and you're not sure how to handle all that's coming at you . . .

The Lord helps the fallen and lifts those bent beneath their loads.

   Psalm 145:14

When you go through deep waters, I will be with you. When you go through rivers of difficulty, you will not drown. When you walk through the fire of oppression, you will not be burned up; the flames will not consume you.

   Isaiah 43:2

All praise to God, the Father of our Lord Jesus Christ. God is our merciful Father and the source of all comfort.
2 Corinthians 1:3

DELIVERANCE

When you wonder if God will rescue you . . .

Don't be afraid. Just stand still and watch the LORD rescue you. . . . The LORD himself will fight for you.
Exodus 14:13-14

The angel of the LORD is a guard; he surrounds and defends all who fear him.
Psalm 34:7

DEPRESSION

When happiness seems a distant memory . . .

The LORD is close to the brokenhearted; he rescues those whose spirits are crushed.
Psalm 34:18

As soon as I pray, you answer me; you encourage me by giving me strength. . . . Though I am surrounded by troubles, . . . you reach out your hand, and the power of your right hand saves me.
Psalm 138:3, 7

When circumstances seem hopeless . . .

I know the LORD is always with me. I will not be shaken,
for he is right beside me. No wonder my heart is glad, and
I rejoice. My body rests in safety. For you will not leave my
soul among the dead or allow your holy one to rot in the
grave. You will show me the way of life, granting me the joy
of your presence and the pleasures of living with you forever.

Psalm 16:8-11

When you feel completely alone . . .

I can never escape from your Spirit! I can never get away from
your presence! . . . Even in darkness I cannot hide from you.
To you the night shines as bright as day. Darkness and light
are the same to you.

Psalm 139:7, 12

DESIRES

**When you really want to love, serve, and honor God
more . . .**

If you look for me wholeheartedly, you will find me.

Jeremiah 29:13

I will give you a new heart, and I will put a new spirit in
you. I will take out your stony, stubborn heart and give you
a tender, responsive heart.

Ezekiel 36:26

When we were controlled by our old nature, sinful desires were at work within us, and . . . produced a harvest of sinful deeds. . . . But now we . . . are no longer captive to [the law's] power. Now we can serve God, not in the old way . . . but in the new way of living in the Spirit.

Romans 7:5-6

DISCIPLINE

When godly living doesn't seem worth the reward . . .

Think about it: Just as a parent disciplines a child, the LORD your God disciplines you for your own good.

Deuteronomy 8:5

Joyful are those you discipline, LORD, those you teach with your instructions.

Psalm 94:12

All athletes are disciplined in their training. They do it to win a prize that will fade away, but we do it for an eternal prize.

1 Corinthians 9:25

When following God's commands seems too hard . . .

Our earthly fathers disciplined us for a few years, doing the best they knew how. But God's discipline is always good for us, so that we might share in his holiness. No discipline is enjoyable while it is happening—it's painful! But afterward there will be a peaceful harvest of right living for those who are trained in this way.

Hebrews 12:10-11

DOUBT

When you're feeling uncertain about God . . .

When doubts filled my mind, your comfort gave me renewed hope and cheer.
Psalm 94:19

Blessed are those who trust in the LORD and have made the LORD their hope and confidence.
Jeremiah 17:7

When you doubt that your faith is enough . . .

I give them eternal life, and they will never perish. No one can snatch them away from me, for my Father has given them to me, and he is more powerful than anyone else. No one can snatch them from the Father's hand.
John 10:28-29

If you confess with your mouth that Jesus is Lord and believe in your heart that God raised him from the dead, you will be saved.
Romans 10:9

When you're facing the impossible . . .

With God everything is possible.
Matthew 19:26

What is impossible for people is possible with God.
Luke 18:27

When circumstances cause you to question your faith . . .

These trials will show that your faith is genuine. It is being tested as fire tests and purifies gold—though your faith is far more precious than mere gold. So when your faith remains strong through many trials, it will bring you much praise and glory and honor on the day when Jesus Christ is revealed to the whole world.

1 Peter 1:7

EMPTINESS

When you long to fill the emptiness deep inside you . . .

Jesus replied, "Anyone who drinks this water will soon become thirsty again. But those who drink the water I give will never be thirsty again. It becomes a fresh, bubbling spring within them, giving them eternal life."

John 4:13-14

May you experience the love of Christ, though it is too great to understand fully. Then you will be made complete with all the fullness of life and power that comes from God.

Ephesians 3:19

ENDURANCE

When your own efforts don't seem to be enough . . .

I am certain that God, who began the good work within you, will continue his work until it is finally finished on the day when Christ Jesus returns.

Philippians 1:6

God is working in you, giving you the desire and the power to do what pleases him.

Philippians 2:13

When you're just barely hanging on . . .

God blesses those who patiently endure testing and temptation. Afterward they will receive the crown of life that God has promised to those who love him.

James 1:12

When you need the willpower and energy to keep going . . .

If we endure hardship, we will reign with him.

2 Timothy 2:12

You know that when your faith is tested, your endurance has a chance to grow. So let it grow, for when your endurance is fully developed, you will be perfect and complete, needing nothing.

James 1:3-4

ENERGY

When you've lost your enthusiasm . . .

Let's not get tired of doing what is good. At just the right time we will reap a harvest of blessing if we don't give up.

Galatians 6:9

When you are exhausted . . .

He gives power to the weak and strength to the powerless.
Even youths will become weak and tired, and young men will
fall in exhaustion. But those who trust in the LORD will find
new strength. They will soar high on wings like eagles. They
will run and not grow weary. They will walk and not faint.
  Isaiah 40:29-31

ETERNAL LIFE

When you want to know how to live forever with God . . .

God loved the world so much that he gave his one and only
Son, so that everyone who believes in him will not perish but
have eternal life.
  John 3:16

Jesus [said], "I am the resurrection and the life. Anyone who
believes in me will live, even after dying. Everyone who lives
in me and believes in me will never ever die."
  John 11:25-26

I have written this to you who believe in the name of the Son
of God, so that you may know you have eternal life.
  1 John 5:13

When you wonder what you will be doing in heaven . . .

No eye has seen, no ear has heard, and no mind has imagined
what God has prepared for those who love him.
  1 Corinthians 2:9

When you need to know that the promise of eternal life makes a difference here and now . . .

If any of you wants to be my follower, you must turn from your selfish ways, take up your cross, and follow me. If you try to hang on to your life, you will lose it. But if you give up your life for my sake and for the sake of the Good News, you will save it.

Mark 8:34-35

We know that God causes everything to work together for the good of those who love God and are called according to his purpose for them.

Romans 8:28

When your faith remains strong through many trials, it will bring you much praise and glory and honor on the day when Jesus Christ is revealed to the whole world.

1 Peter 1:7

EXAMPLE

When you need motivation to be a good example to those around you . . .

Let your good deeds shine out for all to see, so that everyone will praise your heavenly Father.

Matthew 5:16

Take a new grip with your tired hands and strengthen your weak knees. Mark out a straight path for your feet so that those who are weak and lame will not fall but become strong.

Hebrews 12:12-13

∝ FAILURE

When you keep making the same mistakes . . .

The faithful love of the LORD never ends! His mercies
never cease.
Lamentations 3:22

When you're feeling you'll never measure up . . .

Not a single sparrow can fall to the ground without your
Father knowing it. And the very hairs on your head are all
numbered. So don't be afraid; you are more valuable to God
than a whole flock of sparrows.
Matthew 10:29-31

God has not given us a spirit of fear and timidity, but of
power, love, and self-discipline.
2 Timothy 1:7

When you're ready to try again . . .

[The Lord said,] "My grace is all you need. My power
works best in weakness." So now I am glad to boast about
my weaknesses, so that the power of Christ can work
through me.
2 Corinthians 12:9

Forgetting the past and looking forward to what lies
ahead, I press on to reach the end of the race and receive
the heavenly prize for which God, through Christ Jesus,
is calling us.
Philippians 3:13-14

FAITH

When you wonder what faith really is . . .

Faith is the confidence that what we hope for will actually happen; it gives us assurance about things we cannot see.

Hebrews 11:1

When you question the power of having faith in God . . .

Have faith in God. I tell you the truth, you can say to this mountain, "May you be lifted up and thrown into the sea," and it will happen. But you must really believe it will happen and have no doubt in your heart.

Mark 11:22-23

Those who listen to my message and believe in God who sent me have eternal life. They will never be condemned for their sins, but they have already passed from death into life.

John 5:24

When you want your faith to grow . . .

Just as you accepted Christ Jesus as your Lord, you must continue to follow him. Let your roots grow down into him, and let your lives be built on him. Then your faith will grow strong in the truth you were taught, and you will overflow with thankfulness.

Colossians 2:6-7

When you need assurance of what faith leads to . . .

I have fought the good fight, I have finished the race, and I have remained faithful. And now the prize awaits me—the crown of righteousness, which the Lord, the righteous Judge, will give me on the day of his return. And the prize is not just for me but for all who eagerly look forward to his appearing.
2 Timothy 4:7-8

There is a special rest still waiting for the people of God.
Hebrews 4:9

Look, God's home is now among his people! He will live with them, and they will be his people. God himself will be with them. He will wipe every tear from their eyes, and there will be no more death or sorrow or crying or pain. All these things are gone forever.
Revelation 21:3-4

FAITHFULNESS

When you wonder if anyone is trustworthy . . .

O LORD, God of Israel, there is no God like you in all of heaven above or on the earth below. You keep your covenant and show unfailing love to all who walk before you in wholehearted devotion.
1 Kings 8:23

The mountains may move and the hills disappear, but even then my faithful love for you will remain.
Isaiah 54:10

If we are unfaithful, he remains faithful, for he cannot deny who he is.
2 Timothy 2:13

When you want to see the results of faithful living . . .

You will keep in perfect peace all who trust in you, all whose thoughts are fixed on you!
Isaiah 26:3

The Holy Spirit produces this kind of fruit in our lives: love, joy, peace, patience, kindness, goodness, faithfulness, gentleness, and self-control.
Galatians 5:22-23

If we are faithful to the end, trusting God just as firmly as when we first believed, we will share in all that belongs to Christ.
Hebrews 3:14

If you remain faithful even when facing death, I will give you the crown of life.
Revelation 2:10

FAMILY

When you want to leave behind a spiritual heritage . . .

Praise the LORD! How joyful are those who fear the LORD and delight in obeying his commands. Their children will be successful everywhere; an entire generation of godly people will be blessed . . . , and their good deeds will last forever.
Psalm 112:1-3

The godly walk with integrity; blessed are their children who follow them.
Proverbs 20:7

My Spirit will not leave them, and neither will these words I have given you. They will be on your lips and on the lips of your children and your children's children forever. I, the LORD, have spoken!
Isaiah 59:21

When you long to be a part of a family . . .

Anyone who does the will of my Father in heaven is my brother and sister and mother!
Matthew 12:50

God decided in advance to adopt us into his own family by bringing us to himself through Jesus Christ. This is what he wanted to do, and it gave him great pleasure.
Ephesians 1:5

FAVOR WITH GOD

When you want God to smile on you . . .

Never let loyalty and kindness leave you! Tie them around your neck as a reminder. Write them deep within your heart. Then you will find favor with both God and people, and you will earn a good reputation.
Proverbs 3:3-4

The LORD your God is living among you. He is a mighty savior. He will take delight in you with gladness. With his love, he will calm all your fears. He will rejoice over you with joyful songs.
Zephaniah 3:17

‿ FEAR

When your heart is anxious . . .

He will cover you. . . . He will shelter you with his wings. His
faithful promises are your armor and protection. Do not be
afraid of the terrors of the night, nor the arrow that flies in
the day. . . . Though a thousand fall at your side, though ten
thousand are dying around you, . . . if you make the LORD
your refuge, if you make the Most High your shelter, no evil
will conquer you. . . . For he will order his angels to protect
you wherever you go. They will hold you up with their hands.
Psalm 91:4-5, 7, 9-12

All who listen to me will live in peace, untroubled by fear
of harm.
Proverbs 1:33

When you're feeling alone and vulnerable . . .

God is our refuge and strength, always ready to help in times
of trouble. So we will not fear when earthquakes come and
the mountains crumble into the sea.
Psalm 46:1-2

Don't be afraid, for I am with you. Don't be discouraged,
for I am your God. I will strengthen you and help you.
I will hold you up with my victorious right hand.
Isaiah 41:10

When you must confront your fears . . .

Do not be afraid or discouraged, for the LORD will personally
go ahead of you. He will be with you; he will neither fail you
nor abandon you.
Deuteronomy 31:8

See, God has come to save me. I will trust in him and not be afraid. The LORD GOD is my strength and my song; he has given me victory.

Isaiah 12:2

FORGIVENESS

When someone has wronged you . . .

If you forgive those who sin against you, your heavenly Father will forgive you.

Matthew 6:14

When you are praying, first forgive anyone you are holding a grudge against, so that your Father in heaven will forgive your sins, too.

Mark 11:25

When you're feeling ashamed of something . . .

Finally, I confessed all my sins to you and stopped trying to hide my guilt. I said to myself, "I will confess my rebellion to the LORD." And you forgave me! All my guilt is gone.

Psalm 32:5

Fear not; you will no longer live in shame. Don't be afraid; there is no more disgrace for you. You will no longer remember the shame of your youth.

Isaiah 54:4

When you question if God will forgive you . . .

The sacrifice you desire is a broken spirit. You will not reject a broken and repentant heart, O God.

Psalm 51:17

O Lord, you are so good, so ready to forgive, so full of unfailing love for all who ask for your help.

Psalm 86:5

[The Lord says,] Though your sins are like scarlet, I will make them as white as snow. Though they are red like crimson, I will make them as white as wool.

Isaiah 1:18

Everyone has sinned; we all fall short of God's glorious standard. Yet God, with undeserved kindness, declares that we are righteous. He did this through Christ Jesus when he freed us from the penalty for our sins.

Romans 3:23-24

FRIENDS

When you need a real friend . . .

The LORD is a friend to those who fear him.

Psalm 25:14

[Jesus said,] "I no longer call you slaves. . . . Now you are my friends."

John 15:15

If we are living in the light, as God is in the light, then we have fellowship with each other, and the blood of Jesus, his Son, cleanses us from all sin.

1 John 1:7

ᴗ FUTURE

When you're afraid of things to come . . .

The LORD directs our steps, so why try to understand
everything along the way?
Proverbs 20:24

"I know the plans I have for you," says the LORD. "They are
plans for good and not for disaster, to give you a future and
a hope."
Jeremiah 29:11

Don't worry about tomorrow, for tomorrow will bring its own
worries. Today's trouble is enough for today.
Matthew 6:34

When you're planning for the future . . .

The LORD says, "I will guide you along the best pathway for
your life. I will advise you and watch over you."
Psalm 32:8

You guide me with your counsel, leading me to a glorious
destiny.
Psalm 73:24

Trust in the LORD with all your heart; do not depend on your
own understanding. Seek his will in all you do, and he will
show you which path to take.
Proverbs 3:5-6

GIVING

When finances are tight . . .

If you give even a cup of cold water to one of the least of my
followers, you will surely be rewarded.
   Matthew 10:42

Give in proportion to what you have. Whatever you give is
acceptable if you give it eagerly.
   2 Corinthians 8:11-12

You must each decide in your heart how much to give. And
don't give reluctantly or in response to pressure. "For God
loves a person who gives cheerfully." And God will generously
provide all you need. Then you will always have everything
you need and plenty left over to share with others.
   2 Corinthians 9:7-8

When you see an opportunity to help . . .

The generous will prosper; those who refresh others will
themselves be refreshed.
   Proverbs 11:25

Whoever gives to the poor will lack nothing, but those who
close their eyes to poverty will be cursed.
   Proverbs 28:27

When you feel you have nothing to offer . . .

Feed the hungry, and help those in trouble. Then your light
will shine out from the darkness, and the darkness around you
will be as bright as noon.
   Isaiah 58:10

When you're struggling with stinginess . . .

"Bring all the tithes into the storehouse so there will be enough food in my Temple. If you do," says the LORD of Heaven's Armies, "I will open the windows of heaven for you. I will pour out a blessing so great you won't have enough room to take it in! Try it! Put me to the test!"

Malachi 3:10

Give, and you will receive. Your gift will return to you in full—pressed down, shaken together to make room for more, running over, and poured into your lap. The amount you give will determine the amount you get back.

Luke 6:38

Remember this—a farmer who plants only a few seeds will get a small crop. But the one who plants generously will get a generous crop.

2 Corinthians 9:6

GOD'S LOVE

When you think God won't love you anymore . . .

Your unfailing love, O LORD, is as vast as the heavens; your faithfulness reaches beyond the clouds. Your righteousness is like the mighty mountains, your justice like the ocean depths. You care for people and animals alike, O LORD.

Psalm 36:5-6

God loved the world so much that he gave his one and only Son, so that everyone who believes in him will not perish but have eternal life.

John 3:16

I am convinced that nothing can ever separate us from
God's love. Neither death nor life, neither angels nor
demons, neither our fears for today nor our worries about
tomorrow—not even the powers of hell can separate us
from God's love. No power in the sky above or in the earth
below—indeed, nothing in all creation will ever be able to
separate us from the love of God that is revealed in Christ
Jesus our Lord.

Romans 8:38-39

May you have the power to understand, as all God's people
should, how wide, how long, how high, and how deep his love
is. May you experience the love of Christ, though it is too great
to understand fully. Then you will be made complete with all
the fullness of life and power that comes from God.

Ephesians 3:18-19

GRACE

When you wonder if God can possibly still want you . . .

The wages of sin is death, but the free gift of God is eternal
life through Christ Jesus our Lord.

Romans 6:23

God saved you by his grace when you believed. And you can't
take credit for this; it is a gift from God.

Ephesians 2:8

Now he has reconciled you to himself through the death
of Christ. . . . As a result, he has brought you into his own
presence, and you are holy and blameless as you stand before
him without a single fault.

Colossians 1:22

GRIEF

When your heart is breaking . . .

He heals the brokenhearted and bandages their wounds.
Psalm 147:3

When life seems empty after a great loss . . .

I cried out to you, O LORD. I begged the Lord for mercy. . . .
You have turned my mourning into joyful dancing. You have
taken away my clothes of mourning and clothed me with joy,
that I might sing praises to you and not be silent.
Psalm 30:8, 11-12

Let all that I am wait quietly before God, for my hope is in
him. He alone is my rock and my salvation, my fortress where
I will not be shaken.
Psalm 62:5-6

When doubts filled my mind, your comfort gave me renewed
hope and cheer.
Psalm 94:19

I pray that God, the source of hope, will fill you completely with
joy and peace because you trust in him. Then you will overflow
with confident hope through the power of the Holy Spirit.
Romans 15:13

**When your hurt is so deep you don't even know what to
say to God . . .**

The Holy Spirit helps us in our weakness. . . . The Holy Spirit
prays for us with groanings that cannot be expressed in words.
And the Father who knows all hearts knows what the Spirit is
saying, for the Spirit pleads for us believers in harmony with
God's own will.
Romans 8:26-27

GUIDANCE

When you're feeling lost . . .

You see me when I travel and when I rest at home. You know everything I do.
Psalm 139:3

Seek his will in all you do, and he will show you which path to take.
Proverbs 3:6

When the right choice isn't clear . . .

The LORD says, "I will guide you along the best pathway for your life. I will advise you and watch over you."
Psalm 32:8

My child, listen to what I say, and treasure my commands.
. . . Then you will understand what is right, just, and fair, and you will find the right way to go.
Proverbs 2:1, 9

When you're not sure where to turn for guidance . . .

Your word is a lamp to guide my feet and a light for my path.
Psalm 119:105

HEALING

When your body is sick . . .

My health may fail, and my spirit may grow weak, but God remains the strength of my heart; he is mine forever.
Psalm 73:26

O LORD, if you heal me, I will be truly healed; if you save me, I will be truly saved. My praises are for you alone!

Jeremiah 17:14

When your soul needs to be restored . . .

I will never forget your commandments, for by them you give me life.

Psalm 119:93

For you who fear my name, the Sun of Righteousness will rise with healing in his wings. And you will go free, leaping with joy like calves let out to pasture.

Malachi 4:2

He personally carried our sins in his body on the cross so that we can be dead to sin and live for what is right. By his wounds you are healed.

1 Peter 2:24

HEAVEN

When you want a taste of heaven on earth . . .

Oh, the joys of those who do not follow the advice of the wicked, or stand around with sinners, or join in with mockers. But they delight in the law of the LORD, meditating on it day and night.

Psalm 1:1-2

Surely your goodness and unfailing love will pursue me all the days of my life, and I will live in the house of the LORD forever.

Psalm 23:6

Love will last forever! . . . Now we see things imperfectly, like puzzling reflections in a mirror, but then we will see everything with perfect clarity. . . . But . . . three things will last forever—faith, hope, and love—and the greatest of these is love.

1 Corinthians 13:8, 12-13

When life makes you weary . . .

No eye has seen, no ear has heard, and no mind has imagined what God has prepared for those who love him.

1 Corinthians 2:9

This world is not our permanent home; we are looking forward to a home yet to come.

Hebrews 13:14

We are looking forward to the new heavens and new earth he has promised, a world filled with God's righteousness.

2 Peter 3:13

I heard a loud shout from the throne, saying, "Look, God's home is now among his people! He will live with them, and they will be his people. God himself will be with them. He will wipe every tear from their eyes, and there will be no more death or sorrow or crying or pain. All these things are gone forever."

Revelation 21:3-4

HELP

When you can't do it alone . . .

The LORD is my strength and shield. I trust him with all my heart. He helps me, and my heart is filled with joy. I burst out in songs of thanksgiving.

Psalm 28:7

[The Lord said,] "My grace is all you need. My power works best in weakness." So now I am glad to boast about my weaknesses, so that the power of Christ can work through me.

2 Corinthians 12:9

We can say with confidence, "The LORD is my helper, so I will have no fear. What can mere people do to me?"

Hebrews 13:6

When you think you're beyond help . . .

When we were utterly helpless, Christ came at just the right time and died for us sinners.

Romans 5:6

HOME

When you want your home to be a place of blessing . . .

Unless the LORD builds a house, the work of the builders is wasted.

Psalm 127:1

The LORD . . . blesses the home of the upright.

Proverbs 3:33

The house of the wicked will be destroyed, but the tent of the godly will flourish.

Proverbs 14:11

HOPE

When your expectations have been disappointed . . .

The LORD watches over those who fear him, those who rely
on his unfailing love. He rescues them. . . . We put our hope
in the LORD. He is our help and our shield.

Psalm 33:18-20

Take delight in the LORD, and he will give you your heart's
desires. Commit everything you do to the LORD. Trust him,
and he will help you.

Psalm 37:4-5

When you're wondering what to look forward to . . .

Wisdom is sweet to your soul. If you find it, you will have
a bright future, and your hopes will not be cut short.

Proverbs 24:14

This is the secret: Christ lives in you. This gives you assurance
of sharing his glory.

Colossians 1:27

Think clearly and exercise self-control. Look forward to the
gracious salvation that will come to you when Jesus Christ is
revealed to the world.

1 Peter 1:13

**When you need more confidence that Jesus' message
is true . . .**

I have told you all this so that you may have peace in me.
Here on earth you will have many trials and sorrows. But take
heart, because I have overcome the world.

John 16:33

God has given both his promise and his oath. These two things are unchangeable because it is impossible for God to lie. Therefore, we who have fled to him for refuge can have great confidence as we hold to the hope that lies before us. This hope is a strong and trustworthy anchor for our souls. It leads us through the curtain into God's inner sanctuary.

Hebrews 6:18-19

Through Christ you have come to trust in God. And you have placed your faith and hope in God because he raised Christ from the dead and gave him great glory.

1 Peter 1:21

HOSPITALITY

When you hesitate to befriend someone in need . . .

I was hungry, and you fed me. I was thirsty, and you gave me a drink. I was a stranger, and you invited me into your home. I was naked, and you gave me clothing. I was sick, and you cared for me. I was in prison, and you visited me.

Matthew 25:35-36

Don't forget to show hospitality to strangers, for some who have done this have entertained angels without realizing it!

Hebrews 13:2

HUNGER FOR GOD

When the things of this world cannot satisfy your deepest longings . . .

He satisfies the thirsty and fills the hungry with good things.

Psalm 107:9

Jesus replied, "I am the bread of life. Whoever comes to me will never be hungry again. Whoever believes in me will never be thirsty."

John 6:35

When you wonder if you can find the God you long for . . .

If you search for [God] with all your heart and soul, you will find him.

Deuteronomy 4:29

HURTS/HURTING

When you need assurance that your hurts won't last forever . . .

The LORD is close to the brokenhearted; he rescues those whose spirits are crushed.

Psalm 34:18

God blesses those who mourn, for they will be comforted.

Matthew 5:4

We believers also groan, even though we have the Holy Spirit within us as a foretaste of future glory, for we long for our bodies to be released from sin and suffering. We, too, wait with eager hope for the day when God will give us our full rights as his adopted children, including the new bodies he has promised us.

Romans 8:23

We don't look at the troubles we can see now; rather, we fix our gaze on things that cannot be seen. For the things we see now will soon be gone, but the things we cannot see will last forever.

2 Corinthians 4:18

INJUSTICE

When you are frustrated by all the injustice in the world . . .

The righteous LORD loves justice. The virtuous will see
his face.
Psalm 11:7

Let the trees of the forest rustle with praise before the LORD,
for he is coming! He is coming to judge the earth. He will
judge the world with justice, and the nations with his truth.
Psalm 96:12-13

Those who plant injustice will harvest disaster, and their reign
of terror will come to an end.
Proverbs 22:8

He will judge everyone according to what they have done.
Romans 2:6

I saw a new heaven and a new earth, for the old heaven and
the old earth had disappeared. . . . And I saw the holy city,
the new Jerusalem, coming down from God out of heaven.
. . . Nothing evil will be allowed to enter, . . . but only those
whose names are written in the Lamb's Book of Life.
Revelation 21:1-2, 27

INSECURITY

When you haven't put your trust in God . . .

Those who trust in the LORD are as secure as Mount Zion;
they will not be defeated but will endure forever.
Psalm 125:1

Those who fear the LORD are secure; he will be a refuge for their children.
Proverbs 14:26

Teach those who are rich in this world not to be proud and not to trust in their money, which is so unreliable. Their trust should be in God, who richly gives us all we need for our enjoyment.
1 Timothy 6:17

This world is fading away, along with everything that people crave. But anyone who does what pleases God will live forever.
1 John 2:17

INTEGRITY

When you wonder if it's okay to bend the truth a little . . .

Who may worship in your sanctuary, LORD? Who may enter your presence . . . ? Those who lead blameless lives and do what is right, speaking the truth from sincere hearts. Those who refuse to gossip or harm their neighbors or speak evil of their friends. Those who . . . keep their promises even when it hurts. Those who . . . cannot be bribed. . . . Such people will stand firm forever.
Psalm 15:1-5

The LORD rewarded me for doing right. He has seen my innocence. To the faithful you show yourself faithful; to those with integrity you show integrity.
Psalm 18:24-25

Truthful words stand the test of time, but lies are soon exposed.
Proverbs 12:19

If you keep yourself pure, you will be a special utensil for honorable use. Your life will be clean, and you will be ready for the Master to use you for every good work.

2 Timothy 2:21

INTIMACY

When you long to know God deeply . . .

The LORD is a friend to those who fear him. He teaches them his covenant.

Psalm 25:14

The LORD is close to all who call on him, yes, to all who call on him in truth.

Psalm 145:18

The LORD your God is living among you. . . . He will take delight in you with gladness. . . . He will rejoice over you with joyful songs.

Zephaniah 3:17

JOY

When you're feeling drained and your heart seems empty . . .

Oh, the joys of those who do not follow the advice of the wicked, or stand around with sinners, or join in with mockers. But they delight in the law of the LORD, meditating on it day and night.

Psalm 1:1-2

When you obey my commandments, you remain in my love, just as I obey my Father's commandments and remain in his love. I have told you these things so that you will be filled with my joy. Yes, your joy will overflow!
John 15:10-11

When you want to take pleasure in something that will last . . .

The poor will eat and be satisfied. All who seek the LORD will praise him. Their hearts will rejoice with everlasting joy.
Psalm 22:26

I am overwhelmed with joy in the LORD my God! For he has dressed me with the clothing of salvation and draped me in a robe of righteousness. I am like a bridegroom in his wedding suit or a bride with her jewels.
Isaiah 61:10

You have sorrow now, but I will see you again; then you will rejoice, and no one can rob you of that joy.
John 16:22

When our dying bodies have been transformed into bodies that will never die, this Scripture will be fulfilled: "Death is swallowed up in victory. O death, where is your victory? O death, where is your sting?" For sin is the sting that results in death, and the law gives sin its power. But thank God! He gives us victory over sin and death through our Lord Jesus Christ.
1 Corinthians 15:54-57

LOVE

When it is hard to love others . . .

I am giving you a new commandment: Love each other. Just as I have loved you, you should love each other. Your love for one another will prove to the world that you are my disciples.
John 13:34-35

This is real love—not that we loved God, but that he loved us and sent his Son as a sacrifice to take away our sins. Dear friends, since God loved us that much, we surely ought to love each other. . . . If we love each other, God lives in us, and his love is brought to full expression in us.
1 John 4:10-12

When you need to know that love makes a difference . . .

Love is patient and kind. Love is not jealous or boastful or proud or rude. It does not demand its own way. It is not irritable, and it keeps no record of being wronged. It does not rejoice about injustice but rejoices whenever the truth wins out. Love never gives up, never loses faith, is always hopeful, and endures through every circumstance.
1 Corinthians 13:4-7

God is not unjust. He will not forget how hard you have worked for him and how you have shown your love to him by caring for other believers, as you still do.
Hebrews 6:10

MARRIAGE

When you worry that love is not enough . . .

Love never gives up, never loses faith, is always hopeful,
and endures through every circumstance.
  1 Corinthians 13:7

When you feel your needs are ignored . . .

The Lord is a shelter for the oppressed, a refuge in times
of trouble.
  Psalm 9:9

You are my hiding place.
  Psalm 32:7

When you want to strengthen your relationships . . .

This is my commandment: Love each other in the same way
I have loved you. There is no greater love than to lay down
one's life for one's friends.
  John 15:12-13

Above all, clothe yourselves with love, which binds us all
together in perfect harmony.
  Colossians 3:14

MEANING

When you wonder if there's meaning in life . . .

LORD, remind me how brief my time on earth will be. Remind
me that my days are numbered—how fleeting my life is. . . .
[I know] you will show me the way of life, granting me the joy
of your presence and the pleasures of living with you forever.
> *Psalm 39:4; 16:11*

I wait quietly before God, for my victory comes from him.
> *Psalm 62:1*

Imitate God, therefore, in everything you do, because you
are his dear children. Live a life filled with love, following
the example of Christ. He loved us and offered himself as a
sacrifice for us, a pleasing aroma to God. . . . Once you were
full of darkness, but now you have light from the Lord. So
live as people of light! For this light within you produces only
what is good and right and true.
> *Ephesians 5:1-2, 8-9*

MERCY

When you're in need of it . . .

The LORD is compassionate and merciful, slow to get angry
and filled with unfailing love.
> *Psalm 103:8*

The LORD is like a father to his children, tender and
compassionate to those who fear him.
> *Psalm 103:13*

How kind the LORD is! How good he is! So merciful, this
God of ours!
> *Psalm 116:5*

When you realize the depths of God's forgiveness for you . . .

Return to the LORD your God, for he is merciful and compassionate, slow to get angry and filled with unfailing love. He is eager to relent and not punish.
Joel 2:13

Let us come boldly to the throne of our gracious God. There we will receive his mercy, and we will find grace to help us when we need it most.
Hebrews 4:16

When you work to relieve the suffering of others . . .

God blesses those who are merciful, for they will be shown mercy.
Matthew 5:7

MONEY

When you think having more money is the answer to your problems . . .

Riches won't help on the day of judgment, but right living can save you from death.
Proverbs 11:4

Those who love money will never have enough. How meaningless to think that wealth brings true happiness!
Ecclesiastes 5:10

Don't worry about these things, saying, "What will we eat? What will we drink? What will we wear?" These things dominate the thoughts of unbelievers, but your heavenly Father already knows all your needs. Seek the Kingdom of God above all else, and live righteously, and he will give you everything you need.

Matthew 6:31-33

When you want to invest for the future . . .

Wherever your treasure is, there the desires of your heart will also be.

Matthew 6:21

Teach those who are rich in this world not to be proud and not to trust in their money, which is so unreliable. Their trust should be in God, who richly gives us all we need for our enjoyment. Tell them to use their money to do good. They should be rich in good works and generous to those in need, always being ready to share with others. By doing this they will be storing up their treasure as a good foundation for the future so that they may experience true life.

1 Timothy 6:17-19

NEIGHBORS

When you want to be a good neighbor to those living around you . . .

If you love your neighbor, you will fulfill the requirements of God's law.

Romans 13:8

Be careful to live properly among your unbelieving neighbors. Then even if they accuse you of doing wrong, they will see your honorable behavior, and they will give honor to God when he judges the world.

1 Peter 2:12

Don't repay evil for evil. Don't retaliate with insults when people insult you. Instead, pay them back with a blessing. That is what God has called you to do, and he will bless you for it.

1 Peter 3:9

OBEDIENCE

When you think your way of living is best . . .

Do what is right and good in the LORD's sight, so all will go well with you.

Deuteronomy 6:18

The LORD has told you what is good, and this is what he requires of you: to do what is right, to love mercy, and to walk humbly with your God.

Micah 6:8

When you obey my commandments, you remain in my love, just as I obey my Father's commandments and remain in his love. I have told you these things so that you will be filled with my joy. Yes, your joy will overflow!

John 15:10-11

When you are tempted to disobey God's Word . . .

God is faithful. He will not allow the temptation to be more than you can stand. When you are tempted, he will show you a way out so that you can endure.

1 Corinthians 10:13

God is working in you, giving you the desire and the power to do what pleases him.

Philippians 2:13

When you want to have a relationship with God . . .

If you love me, obey my commandments. And I will ask the Father, and he will give you another Advocate, who will never leave you.

John 14:15-16

Keep putting into practice all you learned and received from me—everything you heard from me and saw me doing. Then the God of peace will be with you.

Philippians 4:9

If you look carefully into the perfect law that sets you free, and if you do what it says and don't forget what you heard, then God will bless you for doing it.

James 1:25

Those who obey God's commandments remain in fellowship with him, and he with them. And we know he lives in us because the Spirit he gave us lives in us.

1 John 3:24

OVERWHELMED

When your troubles are piled high . . .

God is our refuge and strength, always ready to help in times of trouble.

Psalm 46:1

When I am overwhelmed, you alone know the way I should turn.

Psalm 142:3

When you're feeling defeated . . .

O LORD, I have so many enemies; so many are against me. . . . But you, O LORD, are a shield around me; you are my glory, the one who holds my head high. . . . Victory comes from you, O LORD.

Psalm 3:1, 3, 8

Can anything ever separate us from Christ's love? Does it mean he no longer loves us if we have trouble or calamity, or are persecuted, or hungry, or destitute, or in danger, or threatened with death? . . . No, despite all these things, overwhelming victory is ours through Christ, who loved us.

Romans 8:35, 37

PAIN

When you are living in chronic pain . . .

Our dying bodies must be transformed into bodies that will never die; our mortal bodies must be transformed into immortal bodies.

1 Corinthians 15:53

I saw a new heaven and a new earth. . . . I heard a loud shout from the throne, saying, "Look, God's home is now among his people! He will live with them. . . . He will wipe every tear from their eyes, and there will be no more death or sorrow or crying or pain. All these things are gone forever."
Revelation 21:1, 3-4

When you wonder if God cares about your pain . . .

I will be glad and rejoice in your unfailing love, for you have seen my troubles, and you care about the anguish of my soul.
Psalm 31:7

When your heart is broken . . .

I weep with sorrow; encourage me by your word. . . . Your promise revives me; it comforts me in all my troubles.
. . . I meditate on your age-old regulations; O LORD, they comfort me.
Psalm 119:28, 50, 52

Let your unfailing love comfort me, just as you promised me, your servant.
Psalm 119:76

God blesses those who mourn, for they will be comforted.
Matthew 5:4

PATIENCE

When God keeps you waiting . . .

I waited patiently for the LORD to help me, and he turned to me and heard my cry.
Psalm 40:1

You are my strength; I wait for you to rescue me, for you,
O God, are my fortress.

Psalm 59:9

The LORD is good to those who depend on him, to those who
search for him.

Lamentations 3:25

When disagreements get you frustrated . . .

May God, who gives this patience and encouragement, help
you live in complete harmony with each other, as is fitting for
followers of Christ Jesus. Then all of you can join together
with one voice, giving praise and glory to God, the Father
of our Lord Jesus Christ.

Romans 15:5-6

When your patience is tested . . .

Patient endurance is what you need now, so that you will
continue to do God's will. Then you will receive all that he
has promised.

Hebrews 10:36

God blesses those who patiently endure testing and temptation.
Afterward they will receive the crown of life that God has
promised to those who love him.

James 1:12

PEACE

When you must face your fears . . .

I will give you peace . . . and you will be able to sleep with no
cause for fear.

Leviticus 26:6

The LORD gives his people strength. The LORD blesses them
with peace.

Psalm 29:11

I am leaving you with a gift—peace of mind and heart. And
the peace I give is a gift the world cannot give. So don't be
troubled or afraid.

John 14:27

When conflict seems inevitable . . .

Turn away from evil and do good. Search for peace, and work
to maintain it. The eyes of the LORD watch over those who do
right; his ears are open to their cries for help.

Psalm 34:14-15

God blesses those who work for peace, for they will be called
the children of God.

Matthew 5:9

Don't worry about anything; instead, pray about everything.
Tell God what you need, and thank him for all he has
done. Then you will experience God's peace, which exceeds
anything we can understand. His peace will guard your hearts
and minds as you live in Christ Jesus.

Philippians 4:6-7

When you desire peaceful living . . .

Those who love your instructions have great peace and do not
stumble.

Psalm 119:165

Oh, that you had listened to my commands! Then you would
have had peace flowing like a gentle river and righteousness
rolling over you like waves in the sea.

Isaiah 48:18

PERFECTION

When you're struggling with your flaws . . .

Everyone has sinned; we all fall short of God's glorious standard. Yet God, with undeserved kindness, declares that we are righteous. He did this through Christ Jesus when he freed us from the penalty for our sins.
Romans 3:23-24

He has reconciled you to himself through the death of Christ in his physical body. As a result, he has brought you into his own presence, and you are holy and blameless as you stand before him without a single fault.
Colossians 1:22

When you set your standards too high . . .

Even perfection has its limits, but your commands have no limit.
Psalm 119:96

[God] said, "My grace is all you need. My power works best in weakness." So now I am glad to boast about my weaknesses, so that the power of Christ can work through me. . . . For when I am weak, then I am strong.
2 Corinthians 12:9-10

PLANNING

When life takes an unexpected turn . . .

God's way is perfect. All the LORD's promises prove true. He is a shield for all who look to him for protection.
Psalm 18:30

You can make many plans, but the LORD's purpose will prevail.

Proverbs 19:21

We know that God causes everything to work together for the good of those who love God and are called according to his purpose for them.

Romans 8:28

When you wish you could see God's purposes . . .

Even the Son of Man came not to be served but to serve others and to give his life as a ransom for many.

Mark 10:45

God has now revealed to us his mysterious plan regarding Christ, a plan to fulfill his own good pleasure. And this is the plan: At the right time he will bring everything together under the authority of Christ—everything in heaven and on earth. Furthermore, because we are united with Christ, we have received an inheritance from God, for he chose us in advance, and he makes everything work out according to his plan. . . . And when you believed in Christ, he identified you as his own by giving you the Holy Spirit, whom he promised long ago. The Spirit is God's guarantee that he will give us the inheritance he promised and that he has purchased us to be his own people. He did this so we would praise and glorify him.

Ephesians 1:9-11, 13-14

When you need to prepare for important future events . . .

Cry out for insight, and ask for understanding. Search for them . . . and you will gain knowledge of God. . . . Then you will understand what is right, just, and fair, and you will find the right way to go.

Proverbs 2:3-5, 9

Trust in the LORD with all your heart; do not depend on your own understanding. Seek his will in all you do, and he will show you which path to take.

Proverbs 3:5-6

POTENTIAL

When you wonder if you can do anything significant for God . . .

I pray that your hearts will be flooded with light so that you can understand the confident hope he has given to those he called—his holy people who are his rich and glorious inheritance.

Ephesians 1:18

All glory to God, who is able, through his mighty power at work within us, to accomplish infinitely more than we might ask or think.

Ephesians 3:20

I can do everything through Christ, who gives me strength.

Philippians 4:13

POWER OF GOD

When you wonder how big God really is . . .

All the nations you made will come and bow before you, Lord; they will praise your holy name.

Psalm 86:9

It is the LORD who provides the sun to light the day and the moon and stars to light the night, and who stirs the sea into roaring waves. His name is the LORD of Heaven's Armies.
   Jeremiah 31:35

Whatever is good and perfect comes down to us from God our Father, who created all the lights in the heavens.
   James 1:17

When you doubt that the power of God can really change a life . . .

With God's help we will do mighty things.
   Psalm 60:12

I am not ashamed of this Good News about Christ. It is the power of God at work, saving everyone who believes.
   Romans 1:16

Just as Christ was raised from the dead by the glorious power of the Father, now we also may live new lives. . . . We know that our old sinful selves were crucified with Christ so that sin might lose its power in our lives. We are no longer slaves to sin.
   Romans 6:4, 6

PRAYER

When you think your worries are too trivial to take to God . . .

I love the LORD because he hears my voice and my prayer for mercy. Because he bends down to listen, I will pray as long as I have breath!
   Psalm 116:1-2

Don't worry about anything; instead, pray about everything. Tell God what you need, and thank him for all he has done. Then you will experience God's peace, which exceeds anything we can understand. His peace will guard your hearts and minds as you live in Christ Jesus.

Philippians 4:6-7

When you wonder if God really hears you . . .

The LORD is close to all who call on him, yes, to all who call on him in truth.

Psalm 145:18

The earnest prayer of a righteous person has great power and produces wonderful results.

James 5:16

The eyes of the Lord watch over those who do right, and his ears are open to their prayers.

1 Peter 3:12

PREPARATION

When you want to get ready for God to work through you . . .

Anyone who listens to my teaching and follows it is wise, like a person who builds a house on solid rock.

Matthew 7:24

May the God of peace . . . equip you with all you need for doing his will. May he produce in you, through the power of Jesus Christ, every good thing that is pleasing to him.

Hebrews 13:20-21

PRESENCE OF GOD

When God seems uninvolved in the world . . .

Look! The virgin will conceive a child! She will give birth to a son, and they will call him Immanuel, which means "God is with us."

Matthew 1:23

The Word became human and made his home among us. He was full of unfailing love and faithfulness. And we have seen his glory, the glory of the Father's one and only Son.

John 1:14

God showed how much he loved us by sending his one and only Son into the world so that we might have eternal life through him. This is real love—not that we loved God, but that he loved us and sent his Son as a sacrifice to take away our sins.

1 John 4:9-10

When you wonder if God wants a relationship with you . . .

Surely your goodness and unfailing love will pursue me all the days of my life, and I will live in the house of the LORD forever.

Psalm 23:6

[The Lord says,] "I have loved you, my people, with an everlasting love. With unfailing love I have drawn you to myself."

Jeremiah 31:3

Because of Christ and our faith in him, we can now come boldly and confidently into God's presence.

Ephesians 3:12

See how very much our Father loves us, for he calls us his children, and that is what we are!

1 John 3:1

When adversity strikes and you need God by your side . . .

I know the LORD is always with me. I will not be shaken, for he is right beside me. . . . You will show me the way of life, granting me the joy of your presence and the pleasures of living with you forever.

Psalm 16:8, 11

When you go through deep waters, I will be with you.

Isaiah 43:2

PRODUCTIVE LIVING

When you desire to be used by God to accomplish his work . . .

The godly will flourish like palm trees and grow strong like the cedars of Lebanon. For they are transplanted to the LORD's own house. They flourish in the courts of our God. Even in old age they will still produce fruit; they will remain vital and green.

Psalm 92:12-14

Yes, I am the vine; you are the branches. Those who remain in me, and I in them, will produce much fruit.

John 15:5

PROTECTION

When you need supernatural care . . .

If you make the LORD your refuge, if you make the Most
High your shelter, no evil will conquer you.

Psalm 91:9-10

He will order his angels to protect you wherever you go. They
will hold you up with their hands.

Psalm 91:11-12

The Lord is faithful; he will strengthen you and guard you
from the evil one.

2 Thessalonians 3:3

PURPOSE

When you need a new vision . . .

Don't copy the behavior and customs of this world, but let
God transform you into a new person by changing the way
you think. Then you will learn to know God's will for you,
which is good and pleasing and perfect.

Romans 12:2

When you wonder what you are here for . . .

If you try to hang on to your life, you will lose it. But if you
give up your life for my sake, you will save it.

Matthew 16:25

My dear brothers and sisters, be strong and immovable.
Always work enthusiastically for the Lord, for you know that
nothing you do for the Lord is ever useless.

1 Corinthians 15:58

When you lose your focus . . .

Turn my eyes from worthless things, and give me life through your word.
Psalm 119:37

I focus on this one thing: Forgetting the past and looking forward to what lies ahead, I press on to reach the end of the race and receive the heavenly prize for which God, through Christ Jesus, is calling us.
Philippians 3:13-14

QUIET

When God's voice is crowded out by the buzz of busyness . . .

This is what the Sovereign LORD, the Holy One of Israel, says: "Only in returning to me and resting in me will you be saved. In quietness and confidence is your strength."
Isaiah 30:15

When you do all the talking and forget to listen to God . . .

I wait quietly before God, for my victory comes from him. . . . Let all that I am wait quietly before God, for my hope is in him.
Psalm 62:1, 5

REFRESHMENT

When your spirits need a lift . . .

The instructions of the LORD are perfect, reviving the soul.
Psalm 19:7

My health may fail, and my spirit may grow weak, but God remains the strength of my heart; he is mine forever.
Psalm 73:26

Your promise revives me; it comforts me in all my troubles.
Psalm 119:50

No power in the sky above or in the earth below—indeed, nothing in all creation will ever be able to separate us from the love of God that is revealed in Christ Jesus our Lord.
Romans 8:39

Let's not get tired of doing what is good. At just the right time we will reap a harvest of blessing if we don't give up.
Galatians 6:9

REGRETS

When your heart is heavy with regret . . .

The high and lofty one who lives in eternity, the Holy One, says this: "I live in the high and holy place with those whose spirits are contrite and humble. I restore the crushed spirit of the humble and revive the courage of those with repentant hearts."
Isaiah 57:15

[The Lord says,] "I will give you a new heart, and I will put a new spirit in you. I will take out your stony, stubborn heart and give you a tender, responsive heart."
Ezekiel 36:26

When you're haunted by your past sins . . .

Repent of your sins and turn to God, so that your sins may be wiped away. Then times of refreshment will come from the presence of the Lord.
Acts 3:19-20

Oh, what joy for those whose disobedience is forgiven, whose sins are put out of sight. Yes, what joy for those whose record the LORD has cleared of sin.
Romans 4:7-8

The kind of sorrow God wants us to experience leads us away from sin and results in salvation. There's no regret for that kind of sorrow.
2 Corinthians 7:10

RESCUE

When you refuse to ask God for help . . .

You rescue the humble, but you humiliate the proud.
Psalm 18:27

When you give in to your sinful desires . . .

Jesus gave his life for our sins, just as God our Father planned, in order to rescue us from this evil world in which we live.
Galatians 1:4

He has rescued us from the kingdom of darkness and transferred us into the Kingdom of his dear Son, who purchased our freedom and forgave our sins.
Colossians 1:13-14

When you desperately need God's help . . .

I waited patiently for the LORD to help me, and he turned to
me and heard my cry. He lifted me out of the pit of despair,
out of the mud and the mire. He set my feet on solid ground
and steadied me as I walked along. He has given me a new
song to sing, a hymn of praise to our God. Many will see
what he has done and be amazed. They will put their trust
in the LORD.
Psalm 40:1-3

The LORD says, "I will rescue those who love me. I will
protect those who trust in my name. When they call on me,
I will answer; I will be with them in trouble. I will rescue
and honor them."
Psalm 91:14-15

REST

When you're tired of crying . . .

I have given rest to the weary and joy to the sorrowing.
Jeremiah 31:25

When you need someone to take care of you . . .

The LORD is my shepherd; I have all that I need. He lets me
rest in green meadows; he leads me beside peaceful streams.
He renews my strength. He guides me along right paths,
bringing honor to his name.
Psalm 23:1-3

Come to me, all of you who are weary and carry heavy burdens,
and I will give you rest.
Matthew 11:28

When hard work leaves you exhausted and you wonder if you can keep going . . .

He gives power to the weak and strength to the powerless. Even youths will become weak and tired, and young men will fall in exhaustion. But those who trust in the LORD will find new strength. They will soar high on wings like eagles. They will run and not grow weary. They will walk and not faint.

Isaiah 40:29-31

Don't be afraid, for I am with you. Don't be discouraged, for I am your God. I will strengthen you and help you. I will hold you up with my victorious right hand.

Isaiah 41:10

There is a special rest still waiting for the people of God. For all who have entered into God's rest have rested from their labors, just as God did after creating the world.

Hebrews 4:9-10

RESURRECTION

When you wonder why the Resurrection matters . . .

Jesus [said], "I am the resurrection and the life. Anyone who believes in me will live, even after dying."

John 11:25

Christ lives within you, so even though your body will die because of sin, the Spirit gives you life because you have been made right with God. The Spirit of God, who raised Jesus from the dead, lives in you. And just as God raised Christ Jesus from the dead, he will give life to your mortal bodies by this same Spirit living within you.

Romans 8:10-11

When you're afraid of dying . . .

I am the resurrection and the life. Anyone who believes in me will live, even after dying. Everyone who lives in me and believes in me will never ever die.

   John 11:25-26

Our earthly bodies are planted in the ground when we die, but they will be raised to live forever. . . . For our dying bodies must be transformed into bodies that will never die; our mortal bodies must be transformed into immortal bodies. Then, when our dying bodies have been transformed into bodies that will never die, this Scripture will be fulfilled: "Death is swallowed up in victory. O death, where is your victory? O death, where is your sting?"

   1 Corinthians 15:42, 53-55

Because God's children are human beings—made of flesh and blood—the Son also became flesh and blood. For only as a human being could he die, and only by dying could he break the power of the devil, who had the power of death. Only in this way could he set free all who have lived their lives as slaves to the fear of dying.

   Hebrews 2:14-15

ROMANCE

When you long for someone to be passionate about you . . .

Surely your goodness and unfailing love will pursue me all the days of my life, and I will live in the house of the LORD forever.

   Psalm 23:6

I will be glad and rejoice in your unfailing love, for you have
seen my troubles, and you care about the anguish of my soul.
   Psalm 31:7

Long ago the LORD said . . . : "I have loved you, my people,
with an everlasting love. With unfailing love I have drawn you
to myself."
   Jeremiah 31:3

Nothing can ever separate us from God's love.
   Romans 8:38

ROUTINE

**When your devotion to God gets lost in your day-to-day
tasks . . .**

My dear brothers and sisters, be strong and immovable.
Always work enthusiastically for the Lord, for you know that
nothing you do for the Lord is ever useless.
   1 Corinthians 15:58

SALVATION

When you wonder if there is any hope for this world . . .

John saw Jesus coming toward him and said, "Look! The Lamb
of God who takes away the sin of the world!"
   John 1:29

[Jesus Christ] is the sacrifice that atones for our sins—and not
only our sins but the sins of all the world.
   1 John 2:2

I saw a new heaven and a new earth. . . . I heard a loud shout from the throne, saying, "Look, God's home is now among his people! He will live with them, and they will be his people. God himself will be with them. He will wipe every tear from their eyes, and there will be no more death or sorrow or crying or pain. All these things are gone forever."

Revelation 21:1, 3-4

When sin makes you feel dead inside . . .

Just as each person is destined to die once and after that comes judgment, so also Christ died once for all time as a sacrifice to take away the sins of many people. He will come again, not to deal with our sins, but to bring salvation to all who are eagerly waiting for him.

Hebrews 9:27-28

When you need to know that salvation can be yours . . .

God loved the world so much that he gave his one and only Son, so that everyone who believes in him will not perish but have eternal life.

John 3:16

If you confess with your mouth that Jesus is Lord and believe in your heart that God raised him from the dead, you will be saved.

Romans 10:9

Remember, he has identified you as his own, guaranteeing that you will be saved on the day of redemption.

Ephesians 4:30

SECURITY

When you need assurance that God will never let you go . . .

God is our refuge and strength, always ready to help in times of trouble.
Psalm 46:1

I cling to you; your strong right hand holds me securely.
Psalm 63:8

Those who trust in the LORD are as secure as Mount Zion; they will not be defeated but will endure forever.
Psalm 125:1

Those who fear the LORD are secure; he will be a refuge for their children.
Proverbs 14:26

All praise to God, the Father of our Lord Jesus Christ, who has blessed us with every spiritual blessing in the heavenly realms because we are united with Christ.
Ephesians 1:3

SELF-CONTROL

When you need help beyond your own willpower . . .

The Holy Spirit produces this kind of fruit in our lives . . . self-control.
Galatians 5:22-23

When you're on the verge of giving in . . .

The temptations in your life are no different from what others experience. And God is faithful. He will not allow the temptation to be more than you can stand. When you are tempted, he will show you a way out so that you can endure.

1 Corinthians 10:13

∾ SIN

When you think you can escape sin's consequences . . .

God will judge us for everything we do, including every secret thing, whether good or bad.

Ecclesiastes 12:14

Everyone has sinned; we all fall short of God's glorious standard.

Romans 3:23

Don't be misled—you cannot mock the justice of God. You will always harvest what you plant.

Galatians 6:7

When you become discouraged in your struggle against sin . . .

I tell you the truth, those who listen to my message and believe in God who sent me have eternal life. They will never be condemned for their sins, but they have already passed from death into life.

John 5:24

The Scriptures declare that we are all prisoners of sin, so we receive God's promise of freedom only by believing in Jesus Christ.

Galatians 3:22

When you fear your mistakes will follow you the rest of your life . . .

He does not punish us for all our sins; he does not deal harshly with us, as we deserve. For his unfailing love toward those who fear him is as great as the height of the heavens above the earth. He has removed our sins as far from us as the east is from the west.

   Psalm 103:10-12

[The Lord says,] "I—yes, I alone—will blot out your sins for my own sake and will never think of them again."

   Isaiah 43:25

When you wonder if there are some who cannot be forgiven . . .

There is forgiveness of sins for all who repent.

   Luke 24:47

We are made right with God by placing our faith in Jesus Christ. And this is true for everyone who believes, no matter who we are.

   Romans 3:22

SPIRITUAL WARFARE

When you feel vulnerable to spiritual attack . . .

Do not let sin control the way you live; do not give in to sinful desires.

   Romans 6:12

Be strong in the Lord and in his mighty power. Put on all of God's armor so that you will be able to stand firm against all strategies of the devil. For we are not fighting against flesh-and-blood enemies, but against evil rulers and authorities of the unseen world, against mighty powers in this dark world, and against evil spirits in the heavenly places. Therefore, put on every piece of God's armor so you will be able to resist the enemy in the time of evil. Then after the battle you will still be standing firm.

Ephesians 6:10-13

Humble yourselves before God. Resist the devil, and he will flee from you.

James 4:7

STRENGTHS/WEAKNESSES

When you come to the end of your own abilities . . .

We now have this light shining in our hearts, but we ourselves are like fragile clay jars containing this great treasure. This makes it clear that our great power is from God, not from ourselves.

2 Corinthians 4:7

My grace is all you need. My power works best in weakness.

2 Corinthians 12:9

STRESS

When life becomes more than you can handle . . .

Give your burdens to the LORD, and he will take care of you.

Psalm 55:22

We were crushed and overwhelmed beyond our ability to endure, and we thought we would never live through it. . . . But as a result, we stopped relying on ourselves and learned to rely only on God, who raises the dead.

2 Corinthians 1:8-9

When you're wondering how to cope with the pressure . . .

I will call to you whenever I'm in trouble, and you will answer me.

Psalm 86:7

As pressure and stress bear down on me, I find joy in your commands.

Psalm 119:143

[Jesus said,] "I have told you all this so that you may have peace in me. Here on earth you will have many trials and sorrows. But take heart, because I have overcome the world."

John 16:33

SUFFERING

When it feels like you have the weight of the world on your shoulders . . .

The LORD helps the fallen and lifts those bent beneath their loads.

Psalm 145:14

When it seems your dark days will never end . . .

You light a lamp for me. The LORD, my God, lights up my darkness.

Psalm 18:28

We are hunted down, but never abandoned by God. We get knocked down, but we are not destroyed. Through suffering, our bodies continue to share in the death of Jesus so that the life of Jesus may also be seen in our bodies.

2 Corinthians 4:9-10

In his kindness God called you to share in his eternal glory by means of Christ Jesus. So after you have suffered a little while, he will restore, support, and strengthen you, and he will place you on a firm foundation.

1 Peter 5:10

He will wipe every tear from their eyes, and there will be no more death or sorrow or crying or pain. All these things are gone forever.

Revelation 21:4

When you're persecuted for your faith . . .

The more we suffer for Christ, the more God will shower us with his comfort through Christ.

2 Corinthians 1:5

Don't be afraid of what you are about to suffer. . . . If you remain faithful even when facing death, I will give you the crown of life.

Revelation 2:10

When you long to be comforted . . .

Sing for joy, O heavens! Rejoice, O earth! Burst into song, O mountains! For the LORD has comforted his people and will have compassion on them in their suffering.

Isaiah 49:13

SURRENDER

When you're ready to give control over to God . . .

If you try to hang on to your life, you will lose it. But if you give up your life for my sake, you will save it.
Matthew 16:25

My old self has been crucified with Christ. It is no longer I who live, but Christ lives in me. So I live in this earthly body by trusting in the Son of God, who loved me and gave himself for me.
Galatians 2:20

SYMPATHY

When you feel like no one understands what you're going through . . .

This High Priest of ours understands our weaknesses, for he faced all of the same testings we do, yet he did not sin. So let us come boldly to the throne of our gracious God. There we will receive his mercy, and we will find grace to help us when we need it most.
Hebrews 4:15-16

TEMPTATION

When the urge is stronger than the strength you have to fight it . . .

The temptations in your life are no different from what others experience. And God is faithful. He will not allow the temptation to be more than you can stand. When you are tempted, he will show you a way out so that you can endure.
  1 Corinthians 10:13

The Lord is faithful; he will strengthen you and guard you from the evil one.
  2 Thessalonians 3:3

When you wonder how many times God will forgive you . . .

"My wayward children," says the LORD, "come back to me, and I will heal your wayward hearts." "Yes, we're coming," the people reply, "for you are the LORD our God."
  Jeremiah 3:22

All glory to God, who is able to keep you from falling away and will bring you with great joy into his glorious presence without a single fault.
  Jude 1:24

THANKFULNESS

When it seems you have nothing to be grateful for . . .

Give thanks to the LORD, for he is good! His faithful love endures forever.
  1 Chronicles 16:34

Thank God! He gives us victory over sin and death through our Lord Jesus Christ.

1 Corinthians 15:57

Be thankful in all circumstances, for this is God's will for you who belong to Christ Jesus.

1 Thessalonians 5:18

TROUBLE

When your problems seem insurmountable . . .

The Sovereign LORD is my strength! He makes me as surefooted as a deer, able to tread upon the heights.

Habakkuk 3:19

We don't look at the troubles we can see now; rather, we fix our gaze on things that cannot be seen. For the things we see now will soon be gone, but the things we cannot see will last forever.

2 Corinthians 4:18

When you wonder if any good can come of your situation . . .

[God says,] "Call on me when you are in trouble, and I will rescue you, and you will give me glory."

Psalm 50:15

We know that God causes everything to work together for the good of those who love God and are called according to his purpose for them.

Romans 8:28

‿ TRUST

When you start to doubt the promises of God . . .

God will do this, for he is faithful to do what he says.
1 Corinthians 1:9

If we are faithful to the end, trusting God just as firmly
as when we first believed, we will share in all that belongs
to Christ.
Hebrews 3:14

Let us hold tightly without wavering to the hope we affirm,
for God can be trusted to keep his promise.
Hebrews 10:23

When you want God to trust you . . .

Never let loyalty and kindness leave you! . . . Then you will
find favor with both God and people, and you will earn a
good reputation.
Proverbs 3:3-4

God is working in you, giving you the desire and the power
to do what pleases him.
Philippians 2:13

When you give God control of your life . . .

Blessed are those who trust in the LORD and have made the
LORD their hope and confidence. They are like trees planted
along a riverbank, with roots that reach deep into the water.
Such trees are not bothered by the heat or worried by long
months of drought. Their leaves stay green, and they never
stop producing fruit.
Jeremiah 17:7-8

TRUTH

When you're uncertain about whether something is or isn't true . . .

Truthful words stand the test of time, but lies are soon exposed.
Proverbs 12:19

All Scripture is inspired by God and is useful to teach us what is true.
2 Timothy 3:16

When the Word of God seems hard to believe . . .

God's way is perfect. All the Lord's promises prove true. He is a shield for all who look to him.
Psalm 18:30

The very essence of your words is truth; all your just regulations will stand forever.
Psalm 119:160

Every word of God proves true.
Proverbs 30:5

When you wonder if telling the truth really matters . . .

Truthful words stand the test of time, but lies are soon exposed.
Proverbs 12:19

If you are faithful in little things, you will be faithful in large ones. But if you are dishonest in little things, you won't be honest with greater responsibilities.
Luke 16:10

VALUES

When you are considering what is truly important in life . . .

Wherever your treasure is, there the desires of your heart will also be.

Luke 12:34

Think about the things of heaven, not the things of earth. For you died to this life, and your real life is hidden with Christ in God. And when Christ, who is your life, is revealed to the whole world, you will share in all his glory.

Colossians 3:2-4

When you really want to live by godly principles . . .

Let the Holy Spirit guide your lives. Then you won't be doing what your sinful nature craves. The sinful nature wants to do evil, which is just the opposite of what the Spirit wants. And the Spirit gives us desires that are the opposite of what the sinful nature desires.

Galatians 5:16-17

WILL OF GOD

When you're confused about the direction your life is going . . .

Commit your actions to the LORD, and your plans will succeed.

Proverbs 16:3

If you look for me wholeheartedly, you will find me.

Jeremiah 29:13

Don't copy the behavior and customs of this world, but let God transform you into a new person by changing the way you think. Then you will learn to know God's will for you, which is good and pleasing and perfect.
Romans 12:2

When you're wondering if God has a plan for you . . .

The LORD directs the steps of the godly. He delights in every detail of their lives.
Psalm 37:23

The LORD will work out his plans for my life—for your faithful love, O LORD, endures forever.
Psalm 138:8

We can make our own plans, but the LORD gives the right answer.
Proverbs 16:1

"For I know the plans I have for you," says the LORD. "They are plans for good and not for disaster, to give you a future and a hope."
Jeremiah 29:11

I am certain that God, who began the good work within you, will continue his work until it is finally finished on the day when Christ Jesus returns.
Philippians 1:6

When your prayers focus on what God desires . . .

We are confident that he hears us whenever we ask for anything that pleases him.
1 John 5:14

WISDOM

When you desire a teachable heart . . .

Come and listen to my counsel. I'll share my heart with you and make you wise.

Proverbs 1:23

Let those who are wise understand these things. Let those with discernment listen carefully. The paths of the LORD are true and right, and righteous people live by walking in them. But in those paths sinners stumble and fall.

Hosea 14:9

When you want to grow in wisdom . . .

Fear of the LORD is the foundation of true wisdom. All who obey his commandments will grow in wisdom.

Psalm 111:10

God gives wisdom, knowledge, and joy to those who please him.

Ecclesiastes 2:26

When your own experience and knowledge fall short . . .

Trust in the LORD with all your heart; do not depend on your own understanding. Seek his will in all you do, and he will show you which path to take.

Proverbs 3:5-6

If you need wisdom, ask our generous God, and he will give it to you. He will not rebuke you for asking.

James 1:5

WITNESSING

When you're not sure how to be a witness for your faith . . .

You are the light of the world—like a city on a hilltop that cannot be hidden. . . . Let your good deeds shine out for all to see, so that everyone will praise your heavenly Father.
Matthew 5:14, 16

Jesus [said], "Come, follow me, and I will show you how to fish for people!"
Mark 1:17

Worship Christ as Lord of your life. And if someone asks about your Christian hope, always be ready to explain it. But do this in a gentle and respectful way. Keep your conscience clear. Then if people speak against you, they will be ashamed when they see what a good life you live because you belong to Christ.
1 Peter 3:15-16

When you're feeling shy about sharing your faith . . .

Those who lead many to righteousness will shine like the stars forever.
Daniel 12:3

I tell you the truth, everyone who acknowledges me publicly here on earth, the Son of Man will also acknowledge in the presence of God's angels.
Luke 12:8

How beautiful are the feet of messengers who bring good news!
Romans 10:15

Faith comes from hearing, that is, hearing the Good News about Christ.
Romans 10:17

WORK

When you feel like the work you do is unappreciated . . .

The LORD will send rain at the proper time from his rich treasury in the heavens and will bless all the work you do.
Deuteronomy 28:12

Be strong and courageous, for your work will be rewarded.
2 Chronicles 15:7

Work willingly at whatever you do, as though you were working for the Lord rather than for people. Remember that the Lord will give you an inheritance as your reward, and that the Master you are serving is Christ.
Colossians 3:23-24

WORRY

When your cares become more than you can handle . . .

Don't worry about anything; instead, pray about everything. Tell God what you need, and thank him for all he has done. Then you will experience God's peace, which exceeds anything we can understand. His peace will guard your hearts and minds as you live in Christ Jesus.
Philippians 4:6-7

Give all your worries and cares to God, for he cares about you.
1 Peter 5:7

When you're stressed about the future . . .

We know that God causes everything to work together for the good of those who love God and are called according to his purpose for them.
Romans 8:28

When the little things become overwhelming . . .

The LORD keeps watch over you as you come and go, both now and forever.

Psalm 121:8

That is why I tell you not to worry about everyday life—whether you have enough food and drink, or enough clothes to wear. Isn't life more than food, and your body more than clothing? Look at the birds. They don't plant or harvest or store food in barns, for your heavenly Father feeds them. And aren't you far more valuable to him than they are? Can all your worries add a single moment to your life?

Matthew 6:25-27

WORTH

When your life seems so insignificant . . .

When I look at the night sky and see the work of your fingers—the moon and the stars you set in place—what are mere mortals that you should think about them, human beings that you should care for them? Yet you made them only a little lower than God and crowned them with glory and honor. You gave them charge of everything you made.

Psalm 8:3-6

When you doubt your worth in God's eyes . . .

God created human beings in his own image. In the image of God he created them; male and female he created them.

Genesis 1:27

What is the price of five sparrows—two copper coins? Yet God does not forget a single one of them. And the very hairs on your head are all numbered. So don't be afraid; you are more valuable to God than a whole flock of sparrows.

Luke 12:6-7

God bought you with a high price.

1 Corinthians 6:20

He has reconciled you to himself through the death of Christ. . . . As a result, he has brought you into his own presence, and you are holy and blameless as you stand before him without a single fault.

Colossians 1:22

❧ FAVORITE VERSES ❧

❧ The Lord Is with You

God has said, "I will never fail you. I will never abandon you."
Hebrews 13:5

❧ You Belong to the Lord

I still belong to you; you hold my right hand. You guide me
with your counsel, leading me to a glorious destiny.
Psalm 73:23-24

❧ Abundant Joy

Joyful are those who have the God of Israel as their helper,
whose hope is in the LORD their God.
Psalm 146:5

❧ May the Lord Bless You

May the LORD bless you and protect you. May the LORD
smile on you and be gracious to you. May the LORD show you
his favor and give you his peace.
Numbers 6:24-26

❧ Peaceful Relationships

Encourage each other. Live in harmony and peace. Then the
God of love and peace will be with you.
2 Corinthians 13:11

The Shepherd's Psalm

The LORD is my shepherd; I have all that I need. He lets me rest in green meadows; he leads me beside peaceful streams. He renews my strength. He guides me along right paths, bringing honor to his name. Even when I walk through the darkest valley, I will not be afraid, for you are close beside me. Your rod and your staff protect and comfort me. You prepare a feast for me in the presence of my enemies. You honor me by anointing my head with oil. My cup overflows with blessings. Surely your goodness and unfailing love will pursue me all the days of my life, and I will live in the house of the LORD forever.

Psalm 23:1-6

The Lord Cares about You

Give all your worries and cares to God, for he cares about you.

1 Peter 5:7

The Lord Is Near

God is our refuge and strength, always ready to help in times of trouble.

Psalm 46:1

The Lord Satisfies

He satisfies the thirsty and fills the hungry with good things.

Psalm 107:9

The Lord Heals

He heals the brokenhearted and bandages their wounds.

Psalm 147:3

The Lord Guides You

Seek his will in all you do, and he will show you which path to take.

Proverbs 3:6

Fruits of the Spirit

The Holy Spirit produces this kind of fruit in our lives: love, joy, peace, patience, kindness, goodness, faithfulness, gentleness, and self-control.

Galatians 5:22-23

Trusting in the Lord

I waited patiently for the LORD to help me, and he turned to me and heard my cry. He lifted me out of the pit of despair, out of the mud and the mire. He set my feet on solid ground and steadied me as I walked along. He has given me a new song to sing, a hymn of praise to our God. Many will see what he has done and be amazed. They will put their trust in the LORD.

Psalm 40:1-3

The Lord Is Your Hope

Why am I discouraged? Why is my heart so sad? I will put my hope in God! I will praise him again —my Savior and my God!

Psalm 42:11

Give Thanks to the Lord

Give thanks to the LORD, for he is good! His faithful love endures forever. Give thanks to the God of gods. His faithful love endures forever. Give thanks to the Lord of lords. His faithful love endures forever. Give thanks to him who alone does mighty miracles. His faithful love endures forever. Give thanks to him who made the heavens so skillfully. His faithful love endures forever.

Psalm 136:1-5

The Lord Watches over You

You know when I sit down or stand up. You know my
thoughts even when I'm far away. You see me when I travel
and when I rest at home. You know everything I do.
Psalm 139:2-3

Do Not Fear

Don't be afraid, for I am with you. Don't be discouraged,
for I am your God. I will strengthen you and help you. I will
hold you up with my victorious right hand.
Isaiah 41:10

The Lord Is Faithful

"The mountains may move and the hills disappear, but even
then my faithful love for you will remain. My covenant of
blessing will never be broken," says the LORD, who has mercy
on you.
Isaiah 54:10

The Lord Gives You Rest

Jesus said, "Come to me, all of you who are weary and carry
heavy burdens, and I will give you rest. Take my yoke upon
you. Let me teach you, because I am humble and gentle at
heart, and you will find rest for your souls."
Matthew 11:28-29

The Lord Helps the Weak

He gives power to the weak and strength to the powerless.
Even youths will become weak and tired, and young men will
fall in exhaustion. But those who trust in the LORD will find
new strength. They will soar high on wings like eagles. They
will run and not grow weary. They will walk and not faint.
Isaiah 40:29-31

The Beatitudes

God blesses those who are poor and realize their need for him, for the Kingdom of Heaven is theirs. God blesses those who mourn, for they will be comforted. God blesses those who are humble, for they will inherit the whole earth. God blesses those who hunger and thirst for justice, for they will be satisfied. God blesses those who are merciful, for they will be shown mercy. God blesses those whose hearts are pure, for they will see God. God blesses those who work for peace, for they will be called the children of God. God blesses those who are persecuted for doing right, for the Kingdom of Heaven is theirs. God blesses you when people mock you and persecute you and lie about you and say all sorts of evil things against you because you are my followers. Be happy about it! Be very glad! For a great reward awaits you in heaven. And remember, the ancient prophets were persecuted in the same way.

Matthew 5:3-12

God Gives Eternal Life

The wages of sin is death, but the free gift of God is eternal life through Christ Jesus our Lord.

Romans 6:23

God Works for Good

We know that God causes everything to work together for the good of those who love God and are called according to his purpose for them.

Romans 8:28

Nothing Can Separate You from God's Love

I am convinced that nothing can ever separate us from God's love. Neither death nor life, neither angels nor demons, neither our fears for today nor our worries about tomorrow—not even the powers of hell can separate us from God's love. No power in the sky above or in the earth below—indeed, nothing in all creation will ever be able to separate us from the love of God that is revealed in Christ Jesus our Lord.

Romans 8:38-39

Christ's Love

Christ will make his home in your hearts as you trust in him. Your roots will grow down into God's love and keep you strong. And may you have the power to understand, as all God's people should, how wide, how long, how high, and how deep his love is. May you experience the love of Christ, though it is too great to understand fully. Then you will be made complete with all the fullness of life and power that comes from God.

Ephesians 3:17-19

Go to God in Time of Need

Let us come boldly to the throne of our gracious God. There we will receive his mercy, and we will find grace to help us when we need it most.

Hebrews 4:16

The Lord Is Your Helper

We can say with confidence, "The Lord is my helper, so I will have no fear. What can mere people do to me?"

Hebrews 13:6

The Lord Never Changes

Jesus Christ is the same yesterday, today, and forever.

Hebrews 13:8

NOTES